THE SHADOW OF DEATH

Stanislaus Eric Stenbock (1860–1895), Count of Bogesund, was born in the South West England to Lucy Sophia Frerichs, an English cotton heiress, and Count Erich Stenbock, who was of a distinguished Swedish family of the Baltic German House of nobility in Reval. He inherited his family's estates in 1885 and returned to live in his manor house at Kolkbriefly for a period before returning to England. In his life he published three volumes of poetry, *Love, Sleep & Dreams*, *Myrtle, Rue and Cypress*, and *The Shadow of Death*, as well as one collection of short stories, *Studies of Death*. He died as a result of alcoholism and opium addiction.

ERIC, COUNT STENBOCK

THE SHADOW OF DEATH

A COLLECTION OF
Poems, Songs and Sonnets

THIS IS A SNUGGLY BOOK

This edition Copyright © 2019
by Snuggly Books.
All rights reserved.

ISBN: 978-1-64525-009-8

This Snuggly Books edition is an unabridged, slightly amended version of that which was published by The Leadenhall Press in 1893.

THE SHADOW OF DEATH

Epilogue to Myrtle, Rue, and Cypress.

> *"Leaves, little leaves*
> *Thy children, thy flatterers thine enemies."*
> —Speech of Marcus Aurulius in
> "Marius the Epicurean."

LEAVES, little leaves, strown on sad Autumn ways,
　　Rent relics of the tender trees in Spring.
Songs, little songs, sad songs of by-gone days,
　　Alas, if the singer have no more heart to sing.

This year, this life; the tree shall not bloom again,
　　What time the leaves are sere and swift to fall;
Yea, and though love be long protracted pain,
　　How should they live who do not love at all?

How shall they live, who have loved, and love not,
    and long to love?
    How shall they sing, who have sung, and have
        nought to sing?
Hath not their life lost all fruit and flower thereof
    And fell frosts sever their short and sterile
        spring?

Leaves, little leaves, waste waifs and stricken strays,
    Farewell, till, like death, the shroud-like snow
        shall fall;
Lives, long-lost loves, and songs of the spent spring
    days,
    Farewell, till snow-like death be the end of all.

Variations on the Same Theme.

I.

SEEK for flowers in the snow, nay, for thou shall find none,
　But phantom fern forms fashioned of the frost;
Weep not for all these things, they are past and gone
　　With the leaves laid low, and the lives and the loves that are lost.
Is it not consolation that in the snow
　　The trees seem well-nigh beautiful and full of peace,
When the leaves are all laid low,
The bitterer blasts have ceased to blow,
　　When the sun smiles silently, shall not then sorrow cease?

Leaves, fallen leaves; ah, my children; ah, my
      belovèd!
   Wind that wailest no more, worn out with
      excess of woe,
Is it worth the while to cherish
Hopes that shall surely perish,
   And to dig for flowers beneath the snow?

II.

Ah, the love, the little love, that you would not
      give,
   The light of life, that the soul ceaseth not to
      crave—
The little love, without which one cannot live,
   And the dead soul drags the live corpse down
      to the grave.
Ah, the soft, the swift, the silent, the shroud-like
      snow.
   Nay, shall I not lay me down and be at peace,
When the leaves are all laid low,
The bitterer blasts have ceased to blow,
   When the shroud is shed around us, shall not
      then sorrow cease?

Leaves, little leaves; ah, my children; ah, my
    belovèd!
  Wind that wailest no more, worn out with the
    excess of woe,
Is it worth the while to cherish
Hopes that shall surely perish,
  And to dig for flowers beneath the snow?

III.

Ah, for is not death shed around us in all the air?
  Doth not Death rise and resound in the
    rhythm and roar of the sea?
Look where thou wilt, thou shalt see Death
    everywhere
  With sad eyes set on the shadow of eternity.
Is not Death's name also written upon the snow?
  Shall we not find in his arms everlasting peace?
When the leaves are all laid low,
The bitterer blasts have ceased to blow,
  When Death kisses our lingering lips, shall not
    then sorrow cease?

Leaves, leaves, leaves; ah, my children; ah, my
    belovèd!

    Wind that wailest no more, worn out with
        excess of woe,
Is it worth the while to cherish
Hopes that shall surely perish,
    And to dig for flowers beneath the snow?

IV.

Hath God condemned me then to live wholly in
    vain?
    Ah, the spring was too short, the summer too
        sad, and the autumn had no joy at all.
Shall not *one* ray of light shine yet ere the ceasing
    of all pain?
    Shall *all* flowers fell without fruit ere the first
        frost fall?
But I said, looking ever forth on the cold, cold
    snow,
    Joy hath not been at all though the end be
        peace.
When the leaves are all laid low,
The bitterer blasts have ceased to blow,
    When *joy* hath ceased to be shall not then
        sorrow cease?

Leaves, little leaves; ah, my children; ah, my
    belovèd!
  Ye are all of you long since dead and gone,
    but I
Am still left here to cherish
Hopes that shall surely perish,
  I have plucked the flower of Death and now I
    am loth to die.

SLAVIC SONGS[1]

I.

"Nje Govorí."

Nay, say no word, I am too nigh to weeping,
   Nor have I heart to look upon thy face,
Speak not at all, but turn thou from me, keeping
   No thought of me, yet grant me this one grace—
But a little while, 'neath the earth I shall be sleeping
   Then lay one flower upon my resting-place.

Then shall I feel thy divine touch thrilling through me,
   Feel the frailest flowers falling, and feel the light

---

[1] These songs are no more Slavic than Mrs. Browning's sonnets are Portuguese. They are only set to Slavic melodies.

Thro' my ashes, of thy sweet eyes turning to me,
  Who, living, were less than ashes in thy
    sight—
Nay, say no word, tho' in life thou didst undo me
  Canst thou deny to the dead this one delight.

II.

Zatsjelúi Menjá do Smjértji.

SAY, shall I bid the moment bide for ever?
    That is so beautiful, or rather say:
"Thou art so beautiful, therefore thine hand sever
    The slender thread and let my life ebb away."
Let my life ebb away, yet kiss me, darling,
    Since the moment cannot stay, and must
      needs pass by,
Kiss me to death, yea, even to death; ah my
    belovèd!
    Ah love! ah life! so long I have longed to die!

I had longed to die, yet said I, "God, in giving
    The gift of life, would surely also give
Some joy to make the life-time worth the living."

Ah love, even now I had liefest cease to live,
I would cease to live, yet do thou slay me, darling,
    Since the moment cannot stay, and must
        needs pass by,
Kiss me to death, yea, even to death; ah my
    belovèd!
    Ah love! ah life! so long I have longed to die!

If I were dead and thou wert to kiss me, darling,
    Oh, from the dead I should surely rise again,
Yet living I were liefer, thou slay me, darling,
    Seeing after this, life were but void and vain,
Say to the moment, "e'en tho' thou be the fairest,
    Thou canst not stay, but also must needs pass
        by."
Kiss me to death, yea, even to death; ah my
    belovèd!
    Ah love! ah life! so long I have longed to die!

III.

Vtsherá Ozhedála Ja Drúga.

I WAITED for thee, my belovèd!
    Waited all through one sweet night of
        spring,
Till tears fell from the wings of the morning,
    And the voices of night ceased to sing.
But I had no joy, my belovèd!
    In the life all around me so fair,
Tho' all Heaven lay open before me,
    What care I, if my love be not there!

How sweet it had been, my belovèd!
    In the music and moonlight of May,
When the nights, wherein dwelleth no darkness,
    Thrill still with delight of the day.
To have wandered, and wandered, and wandered,

    And how sweet to have rested—ah where?
Shall I wander or rest now, belovèd?
    What rest if my love be not there?

I have waited so long, my belovèd!
    Thro' long days and long nights and long years,
In the changing of morning and evening
    Shines no sun thro' the dew-fall of tears—
I have waited too long, I am weary
    And chilled and afraid in the gloom,
I shall not live to see my belovèd,
    But may-be feel his tears on my tomb.

IV.

Ja Vas Ljubíl.

AH sweet! those eyes, that used to be so tender,
    Are grown so cold, as bitter cold as death,
The burnt out ashes fall into the fender,
    None shall revive the flame that perisheth.

So leave me "love," just kiss me one, then turning
    Go forth from me before the fall of day,
It were better "love" to leave the ashes burning,
    Than wait, too late, *till* they are burnt away.

Amor Mysticus.

I.

FROM the east window of my pleasure-house,
There is a forest of trees blossoming,
That stir a little when a Seraph's wing,
In passing over them, makes melody
    Faint fluttering o'er vibrant viol string—
    But from western window steep and sheer,
        The wailing waters of an infinite sea,
        In refluent response of a litany,
Against the casement ever splash and souse.
Even there I dreamed I dwelt with you, my dear,
[1] I dreamed of *you*, but *you* did not dream of *me*.

---

[1] "J'ai rêvé d'elle mais elle n'a pas rêvé de moi."
                      —P. Verlaine.

II.

But when I looked on those mysterious eyes,
    Then spirit choristers began to sing
Of wailing waters and trees blossoming—
Because those eyes are like the melody
    That flutters o'er a vibrant viol string,
Earth seen thro' water, suffused with the shadow
    of fire,
But mostly like mute moonlight on calm sea—
    Oh then! I thought of my dream litany
And offered up my soul in sacrifice.
That in your soul One thought I might inspire,
For *I* loved you, but you did not care for *me*.

III.

And so I prayed that never any word
My love might hear of my soul's travailing—
Nathless I cannot help remembering
How very sad was that long stretch of sea,
And yet how glad were those trees blossoming,
So at that hour when the day was done,
And you, too, knelt in that dim sanctuary,

I, through the wave-beats of that litany,
Prayed—"Though my soul be given to the sword,
"Oh spare my darling, spare mine only one."
I prayed for *you*, but *you* did not pray for *me*.

"Gabriel."

*"Le bercement vague d'une incantation magique
entendue à demi dans un rêve"*

MINE head upon thy lap, love, let me lie,
I am wounded, and without thee I shall die,
Lull me and love me, love! till I am well,
                        Gabriel.

Turn on me sweetly till my soul have ease,
Thine evening eyes, that seem to breathe forth peace,
Wherefrom the tender tears are quick to quell,
                        Gabriel.

Ah! for an everlasting afternoon—
Lift not thine eyes, lest sunset come too soon,

With the long tolling of the vesper bell,
                                      Gabriel.

The sweet, slow, sleepy, solemn sounds that seem
Like incantations half heard in a dream,
Or sad-eyed Siren singing some strange sea spell,
                                      Gabriel.

Sing me to sleep while the long shadows wane,
Sing me the songs of childhood—come again
With thy sweet eyes, that all ill thoughts repel,
                                      Gabriel.

In blessing lay thine hands upon my head,
Ah! would that with the sunset I were dead!
Having lived for one sweet hour, too sweet to tell,
                                      Gabriel.

Living no longer than the lingering light,
Seeing thy sweet eyes slowly sink from sight,
While the slant shadows sound my dying knell,
                                      Gabriel.

Viol d'Amor.

"IT is only the wind, Anastasia!
    Only the wind and the rain,
And the blooming branch of the blackthorn
    That for me shall not bloom again—

"Sing me a song, my sister!
    For I love not the wild wind's moan,
To the Viol d'Amor, Anastasia!
    That is so sweet of tone,
Let me hear thee near, Anastasia!
    I shall soon be quite alone."

"Nay, but close thine eyes, my brother!
    Close thine eyes with thy lashes long,
May be thou wilt sleep, my-darling,
    If I sing thee an old world song,

Of the old times since forgotten,
    Not worth remembering long."

"It is only the wind, Anastasia!
    For now it has ceased to rain,
And a cold moon ray thro' the blackthorn
    Slides right through the window pane.
Her sad song slid on the moonbeam,
    And the viol strings throbbed again."

Rain pearls on the blooming blackthorn,
    The pale moon with silver tips,
To the Viol d'Amor's sad cadence
    The roof-shed rain-fall drips—
A shadow crept thro' the doorway
    And kissed the pale boy on the lips.

The Red Hawthorn.
(Song to Stringed Instrument.)

MY love is gone away,
I have no heart to sing,
I have but this to say,
May is no longer May,
Spring is no longer Spring,
Nor shall I find delight—in anything.

I used to love the May,
Red Hawthorn blossoming,
The fire-lost, flame-red spray,
Because I used to say
Of all the flowers of Spring
This is most like my love—to my imagining.

My love has gone away,
I have no heart to sing.

Oh sad scent of sweet May,
Saddest at fall of day,
Death-scent thro' living Spring;
May is no longer May,
Spring is no longer Spring.

The Death-Watch.

DARLING, would you be sorry
    If you knew that I were dead?
Who loved you above all things,
    Though never word I said.

Did you know dear, that I loved you?
    One day your look was kind,
And one day-oh, so sad, love!
    Were I dead, dear, would you mind?

Eyes! that I dared not look to,
    Lips I that I dared not touch—
Would you pray for me a little,
    Who prayed for you so much?

If passing to my grave, dear,
    On some sad All Souls day—
Oh! where your tears had fallen
    Violets would bloom alway.

Song.

I BUILT a house of cards,
    It was far too fain to fall down,
I said as I picked up each one,
    Through my cross there shall shine no crown.

I built a house for friends,
    I said what could be more dear,
For I knew not that friendship ends,
    And I knew not that you were near.

I built a palace of love,
    But my heart has grown over weak,
Being torn with the pain thereof,
    I am silent and shall not speak.

The Turn-Stile.

WHY dost thou mourn? The days are very few,
    Frail flowers are watered from thine eyelids wet—
Thy tears are far too salt—not like the dew,
    Nor shall thy love return for thy regret—
        O thou that livest on memory!—sleep and forget.

The days are few—'tis not worth while to weep,
    Yet do I doubt that aught might make thee smile—
T'is weariness to wake—better to sleep,
    Yet even to sleep were hardly worth our while,
        Come! let us go!—'tis not far—to life's turn-stile.

Perhaps.

PERHAPS in the long sweet living days of
      spring,
  When the tree-blossoms fall softer than the
    snow
And fields, and floods. and flowers unite to sing,
  Thou wilt wander in the ways we used to go.
Perhaps thou wilt sadden a little, remembering
Some word, some jest, some slight and trivial
     thing,
  Or reach of flowers, that we used to know,
  And thou wilt remember me who loved you so.

Perhaps thou wilt linger a little, loth to part—
  In the long sweet spring-days it is often so,
That sudden tears will to the eyelids start,
  Thinking of things far off, and long ago—
Then I shall bless thee, seeing how sweet thou art,

But a sevenfold sword shall pierce me thro' the
    heart,
  And there shall be no ending to my woe,
  If thou remember me not who loved thee so.

Perhaps thou wilt weep a little for my sake,
  Ah love! I would no sadness thou mightest
    know,
How could I have the cruelty to make,
  Even for one moment, thy priceless tears to
    flow—
Oh, my soul longeth in thy tears her thirst to slake,
Nay, if thou weep not, surely my heart shall
    break—
  I cannot bear that thou should'st forget
    me—no,
  Thou *shalt* remember me who loved thee so.

Fragment.

WEEP for what was not, and what might have been,
    What might have been and has not been at all—
Ah, the snow fell before the grass grew green,
    Ah, sad sweet eyes, that the tears fill and do not fall.

Oh thou wert as soft sunset thro' my days,
    And thro' my nights as sundawn lingering.
I looked on thee and blessed thy words and ways,
    Sad eyes fore-saddened with unseen sorrowing.

I dare not look on thee to say farewell,
    Oh, shall we say that it were better so?
The measure of missed misery, who shall tell,
    Sad eyes that sing long litanies of woe.

Thou wilt remember me when far away,
    Thou *wilt* remember, since thou canst not
        forget,
Thro' my long night and thro' my dreamless day,
    Ah, sad sweet eyes, reflecting all regret.

Ἠράμην σέθεν Ἄτθι πάλαι πότα.
                                Sappho.

DOST thou remember—was it *long* ago?
    How once we wandered hand in hand
  Along the sadness of the sand
And the sea sobbed and the wind wailed with woe.

Dost thou remember—the sea-swallows cry?
    As though nought might assuage their grief
    Or bring them respite or relief—
I held thine hand the closer—thou didst sigh.

Dost thou remember—dost thou wander now
    Along the same untrodden ways
    And think in these sad Autumn days
How once we went together, I and thou?

*"An Mariä Geburt
Ziehen dei Schwalben furt."*

HOW shall I sing—what shall I say
If all my swallows be flown away?
I have little heart to sing to-day.

Swallows that fly to the end of the earth,
Swallows that sway o'er the sea's great girth,
Swallows that fly on Mary's birth.

Loves of the past—songs of to-day,
All with the swallows are flown away,
Nothing on earth may endure or stay.

Oh let thy mourning be turned to mirth,
With the swallows fly away from the earth,
Rejoice and be glad in Mary's birth.

Complies de La Sainte Vierge.

OH! la Vierge Marie
    Donne le sommeil
Espère! chacun qui prie,
   Voit le reveil,
Chacun par toute la nuit
   Voit le vermeil—
Vermeil qui vétit
   L'aube du soleil.
    Espère! par toute la nuit
   Pour le reveil
Car la Vierge Marie
   Donne le sommeil.

To Saint Teresa.

YES, we have heard of thee long before now,
    Pallas Athene with her shield and sword,
And crested helmet on her virgin brow,
    But her words were not as thy word.

Yes, we have heard of thee long time agone,
    Diotima speaking unto Socrates
Words of great wisdom, but of thine, but one
    Word were more worth than hundred-fold of these.

How sweet it is to say the word "Carmél"!
    Sancta Teresa, how my spirit faint:
To think of those who dwelt and those who dwell,
    Thy progeny the prophets and the saints.

Chanson Solaire.

SUNLIGHT, sacred light, and lovely wind of
    the morning,
  There is no delight in the night but only
    delight in thee,
Who, all the sadness of night and terror of dread
    dreams scorning,
Vesteth the mountains with gold, and shimmereth
    along the sea.

Oh! when the sun has arisen—then all the Angels
    in glory
  Say: "Glory to God in the highest and unto
    mankind be peace."
And who is he that shall dare to re-tell the same
    old false story,
  That seekers may seek in vain, and of
suffering that may not cease.

Autumn Song.
(Nocturne.)

I.

WHEN the nights are so cold—belovèd,
    And thy grave not with my tears wet,
Then will I visit thee most—oh, my belovèd,
    In the rapture of regret.

When the days are all haze and mist, belovèd—
    In the lingering leaf-falling sunset,
  I will twine flowers round thy tomb—oh, my belovèd,
    In the luxury of regret.

Autumn Song.
(Vespertine.)

II.

SWEET! how sweet it were to die
    On this placid afternoon
  Before the rising of the moon,
Love! together you and I.
    It is not very much too soon—
      Leaves fall—I and you
        Must die too.

So as not to hear the rushing rain,
So as not to feel the falling snow,
And winter, wild and waste with woe,
At least we shall not see again.
Come, my belovèd, it is time to go—
      Leaves fall—I and you
        Must die too.

Requiem.

BRETHREN! I pray you of your charity
    To pray for one who is not dead, but lives.
  That God among the many gifts He gives,
May give some little gift to such as he—

Who is not dead, nor sleeping, but awake—
    That He might give some slight surcease of
        pain
    To one who cannot render you again
Your spiritual arms for Jesus' sake.

One drop of water just to cool his tongue—
    Ye that are old and seem too full of woe,
  Because 'tis nearly time for you to go,
Oh pray for one who is not old but young.

But children mostly, ye that have the light
  Of heaven still upon your faces fair:
  Oh pray for one who most may need your
    prayer,
Because your angels stand within God's sight.

"All Souls' Even."

BUT a few flowers, just a few
    Upon my grave, that I may see
   That you have sometime thought on me
Who never cease to think on you.

Oh, it is dark, and dank and drear,
   Dismal and dreadful underground,
    Where the wind sighs unpityingly around,
And the rain falls not softly like a tear.

But was there one that loved the dead?
   A faltering footstep went and came,
    Tall tapers flared with flickering flame,
And flowers were laid upon my head.

And so I blessed the gentle day
   When some will turn them from the strife,

    And war of words and lust of life,
To think on old friends passed away.

And so this night I cry to you,
    And bless you that you came to me—
    Who did not ask inordinately—
But a few flowers, just a few.

*"Requiem aeternam
Dona eis Domine
Et lux perpetua luceat eis."*

TEACH us to pray for the belovèd dead,
    Since we are blind and know not what is best.
The still small voice of Silence answering said,
        "Pray for rest."

Oh, my lost love, and shall I therefore pray
    That thou may'st sleep through an eternal night?
The still small voice of Silence answered, "Nay,
        "Pray for light."

Birthday Song.

October 24th, 1891.

THOU wast born when the leaves all fall,
    And the tombs with tears are wet—
All fall, but amongst this all
    Blooms the first violet.

Roses are not yet dead,
    Dahlias for glory shine—
Twine the violets round thine head,
    Their herald Spring-tide be thine!

To have travelled for twenty years—
    Does the way seem somewhat long?
Plenty of time for tears,
    But the time is not over for song.

Chant de Cygne.

IS it the hills that are not high,
    Or the scant verdure of the plain,
I sorrow not to see again—
      Or why
     Is it such pain
        To die?

Limited and familiar sky!
   And earth that I have known so long!
    Surely my hold on you is strong—
      Else why
     Does it seem wrong
        To die?

I have no loves to bid "good-bye,"
   No hands to thrill me at their touch,

And none will miss me very much—
    So why
  Is it sad that such
      As I
    Should die?

Nocturne.

'TIS not the song that dies into a sigh,
    Or flower-twined tomb-stone with the
  singing dove—
For these are nowise meant for me—for I
    Have sung out all my song, loved all my love—
Leave me alone to be sick, leave me alone to die!

'Tis not the desolation and the doom,
    And wail of bitter tears—I want no poetry,
For the dead dullness of the Spiral room
    Are more than I deserve, far more, for why
Should I, whose shaft has withered without bloom,
    Seek fallen flowers and fruit?—leave me alone
      to die!

Expectatio Partûs B. V. M.

THE night was full of fever and unrest,
    The hours went drearily and wearily,
But at the sunrise I arose and blest
    The amber light that shimmered on the sea.

Before, the moon was growing over pale,
    A mystical white mist fell freezingly,
An Angel came and moved away the veil,
    Whose amber footsteps shimmered on the sea.

Gabriel, sent to Mary long ago,
    With flame-like feet bent down adoringly,
Christ shall soon come to ease us of our woe,
    Because thy footsteps shimmer on the sea.

Die Hinterlassenen.

THEY journeyed onward, shadowed by a star.
    But we were far too faint to follow them,
We cried—"Oh, whither go ye? is it far?"
    "Yes—to Bethlehem."

Some spake of Angels singing in the night,
    Of glory and good will, and most of peace;
And how the darkness shone with a great light—
    —But our woe did not cease.

We are still sitting in the shade of Death,
    (The wise men and the shepherds are gone by)
In our lone desolate land, which visiteth
    No day-spring from on high.

Noel.

HE held the world within his hand,
    The sky grew golden when He smiled,
The sea stood still at His command,
                A little child.

Mary and Joseph, only ye
    Could e'er have seen Him when He smiled;
Men saw Him weeping bitterly,
                Your little child.

O love, that casteth out all fear,
On thy straw couch in winter wild,
    Spare for me too one single tear,
                O Little Child.

Sylvesternacht
—To the Old Year.

FAREWELL, thou hast had thy fill
      Of sin and sorrow,
Farewell, shall we fare less ill
      To-morrow.

Go—thou hast had thy share
      Of vain regret,
Shall sunrise seem more fair
      Than sunset.

Washed, thou art not made pure
      With floods of tears,
Shall next year have less to endure
      Than other years?

Left leaves and loves laid low!
        Faith, hope grown cold.
Will a wind less bitter blow
        The crocus gold?

Kings are come from afar,
        Let us follow them—
They say they have seen a star
        In Bethlehem.

May Blossom.
(A Vision.)

I SPRINKLED on my bed to-day,
    Upon my bed of ceaseless pain,
Some of the perfume of red may—
    —I shall not see the spring again.

It seemed, some halo of the moon,
    Which lambent, carmine shadows threw;
The disc was wholly silver soon
    Encircled with a ring of blue.

And in that silvern heart of space,
    Slowly an image did arise,
Thy strange dark hair, thy strange pale fine,
    And thine unfathomable eyes.

But oh! thy face was *very* pale,
    Thine eyes were wilder than of old—
Thou triedst to speak, but speech did fail,
    And darling! how thy lips were cold.

It seemed there fell a red white snow
    Upon my bed of ceaseless pain,
From where the far off hawthorns grow,
    I shall not see the spring again.

Fragment.

OH child, my child, whose eyes are like the light
    Of sunset lessening yet lingering,
Might I not gladden a little in their sight,
    And my sad shadowy Autumn seem like Spring?

Alas! I may not enter Paradise,
    And Spring—ah Spring—was never Spring for me—
Pray but one prayer for me with thy sweet eyes
    And let my soul of thine have charity!

Nocturne.

CHILD, if I say or said
      This litany,
Wilt thou on thy white bed
      Pray for me?

My soul with sin is red,
      Oh pray for me.
Angels stand round thy bed,
      And wait on thee.

Thy soul is white as snow,
      Pray thou for me.
My soul is waste with woe,
      Yet *I* pray for thee.

My prayers have no avail—
      If I pray for thee,
God's grace can never fail
      If thou pray for me.

Mondsee.
(Nocturne.)

SURELY it were a sweeter thing to have,
    Instead of cold, hard, pitiless earth for grave,
Thy waters—Monsea! that thy moonlights lave,
   When the strange shadows sleep beneath thy wave.

When the swans wander thro' the silvern sheen,
    Over the gray-blue place where dwells Undine,
Whose mystical sad eyes are such dark green
   As the moon shining on a Tourmaline.

Lilies, and reeds, and trees, and mountains steep,
    Are all reflected there where I would sleep—
—And oh, thy waters seem so dark and deep,
   When guardian angel stars their vigils keep.

The Passion of Sleep.

Ballade.

HOW sweet it is to fall—
    Waters of grey, green, blue!
Walled with a yielding will
   Your liquid crystal through—
   Here no foot may pursue,
Tho' voices afar may call—
   —Voices afar are few—
       Sleep is the best of all.

World of wormwood and gall,
   Whose myrtle is only rue,
Give me the cypress tall,
   And moon-thrown shadows of yew.
   Let weeping winters strew
Snow on my bed for a pall—
   —This thing alone is true—
       Sleep is the best of all.

Envoi.

Sweet—*how* I dream of you!
    Do you dream of *me* at all?—
If you *did*, would you say too?
        Sleep is the best of all.

Fragment.

Music and Sleep are one, and Love and Death
Are even as their brethren—let us die—
Or let me sleep where thou canst play to me,
Let thy violin-like voice flow over me,
Like oil poured forth upon the savage waves
That beat upon the prow of a dark ship
Which bears a load of shadows of despair.

Prayer.

"O Clemens, O pia, O dulcis Virgo Maria."

O THOU of seven sorrows, list to me—
I, who have many sorrows, call to thee—
Let me have some of thy sweet charity.

Thou, who art wise, forgive my foolishness;
Thou, who art sweet, forgive my bitterness;
Thou, who art gentle, forgive mine ungentleness.

Thou, who art clement, thou who art good and
    sweet,
Turn to the exile, crawling at thy feet,
Thine eyes too full of mercy, and entreat,
God to be merciful from the mercy seat.

Fragment.

"Ad vesperum demorabitur fletus
et ad matutinum laetitia."

GOD said, "I wait," and "shall I longer wait,
"There is one way, although the way be strait,
"That way winds straightly unto Heaven's gate."

I said, "My seed hath fallen among thorns,
"And through sad evenings until joyless morns,
"I did not heed or hear the voice that warns.

"Too sad at eve, at morning to rejoice,
"Mine ears were deafened by the worlds great
      noise.
"Alas! I did not listen to Thy voice."

Sonnet I.
New Year's Night.

OH, the moon shines lugubriously, cold and drear,
A weird, white mist falls freezingly over all,
Shadowy, like a shroud the old year's funeral pall.

The weary, wicked, woeful, worn old year,
    On his dim death-bed now grown almost drear,
        The old sad year, on whom we used to call
        With curses on our lips—now the tears fall,
Why should we weep for what is not worth a tear?

A shrinking from the unfamiliar days,
    The dreamer, who awakening from his dream,
        Is loth to look upon the lorn grey light,
Or as the traveller, travelling on strange ways,
    Is sick at heart, because the strange things seem
        To pain him rather, where he sought delight.

Sonnet II.

TO travel is to die continually,
    To see things at their saddest—passing away—
    The horror of strange faces every day,
And the sad travail of still-born sympathy,
Oh, what is death but this same agony—
    To look upon the sun-lit fields and say,
    "To-morrow shall not be as yesterday."
    Who knows to-morrow what mine eyes may see?

A few wild flowers strewn within the street,
    Is it with tears or with the rain-fall wet?
The few familiar faces we used to greet,
    Small things whereon so little store we set,
Are in this latter day grown strangely sweet
    And sad with the association of regret.

Sonnet III.
Ad Patriam.

LAND, whoso looks upon thee only sees
    The woeful weariness of thy waste ways.
  Wastes that the horror of the horizon hardly
    stays.
Oh melancholy and manifold of maladies
Where the tears fall not, but are fain to freeze,
    In the intolerable darklessness of thy dim days,
    In the intolerable tyranny that weaves and
      weighs
A shrivelled shroud to cover all thy skies.

Ah, the little thing, the swift, the sudden spring,
    The bright, warm days, when life of life grew
      fair,
    And viol-strings vibrated in all the air.

Oh, thrice-accursed land! Thou could'st not bear
That we should have solace of our sorrowing,
So hast thou swathed our spring in thy snows again.

Sonnet IV.
On the Freezing of the Baltic Sea.

WHO hath not lingered a little by the shore?
    Seeking a symbol in the sighing of the sea,
  Floods of vain desire refluent eternally
Ebbs of hopes, lost and again for evermore—
Novelty of horror—thought not conceived before—
    Livid and leaden-hued, lifeless, the solid sea,
    Silently stretching towards infinity,
Ice more fearful than storms, and the great waves roar.

"If the sea sigh not, then shall I die," I said,
    "I have loved the sea for its passion and its pain
      In the world-woe's image seeking a solace of woe,

If the sea sigh not, then surely is all hope dead—"
   And as I cast mine eyes on the sea again,
      One walked upon the waters, sombre,
         solemn, and slow.

Sonnet V.
(Written in Sickness.)

"Ego dixi in dimidio dierum meorum vadam ad portas inferi."

I SAID, "I will go down into the pit,
   Even before the ending of my day."
  So I am fallen weary on the way.
Life shall not leave me loth to part from it.

For the long light outlives the little sweet
   In the sad sojourn of the desolate day,
  But night brings sleep and solace, so I say:
"Give me the cleft pomegranate that I may eat."

But now death dims the light about mine head,
   O let me live, for I were loth to die.
  The old familiar earth and limited sky
Are dear to me, e'en tho' my heart have bled—
Oh let me live and let me love—a lie.

Sonnet VI.

"O vos omnes, qui transitis per viam, attendite et videte si est dolor similis sicut dolor meus."

ALL suffer, but *thou* shalt suffer inordinately.
    All weep, but *thy* tears shall be tears of blood.
I will destroy the blossom in the blood,
Nathless, I will not slay thee utterly—
    Nay, thou shalt *live*—I will implant in thee
        Strange lusts and dark desires, lest any should,
        In passing, look on thee in piteous mood,
For from the first I have my mark on thee.

So shalt thou suffer without sympathy,
And should'st thou stand within the street and
        say:

"Look on me, ye that wander by the way,
If there be any sorrow like to mine."
They shall not bind thy wounds with oil and wine,
But with strange eyes downcast, shall turn from thee.

Sonnet VII.

LET us go home—didst thou not hear a sound?
   A long, low, lispèd laugh—didst thou not hear?
   A wicked whisper echoing in mine ear,
And through the shuddering silence all around,
A growling as of wild beasts underground.
   And so I know mine enemy is near,
   Who dwelleth in the darkness, fraught with fear,
Tracking me ever as a silent hound.

Look down into the river, deep, deep, deep—
   Betwixt our long, dark shadows hand in hand.
   Cast upward from the water—not down from the land.
A shadow fainter than a shade—laugh not nor weep.
Was that the echo of a rock that fell?
But also a louder laugh, hardly hushed in Hell.

Sonnet VIII.

OH—and the darkness grew intolerable,
    And as I looked down the long, low corridor
    I felt another horror, unfelt before.
There was no light there—but may-be the flames of Hell
Cast shadows darker than darkness—palpable—
    It did not walk, yet crept not on the floor,
    And my soul froze within me to the core.
It touched me and It spake—how It spake I cannot tell.

Yea, and It spake to me thus mockingly:
    "Resist me not, with me there is no strife,
    Did'st thou not call upon me, I am come
    To be the Guardian Angel of thine home,
To be a light to lighten all thy life
Henceforth we will dwell together, thou and I."

Sonnet IX.

"The long hours come and go, and come and go."
—Christina Rossetti.

WHAT is the time? what of the time? alas!
    The hours that go and come, and come and go,
    The long-short hours, so swift, so sad, so slow
The turning and returning of the glass
For hours, that linger a little as they pass;
    Or hours, that have not wept out all their woe,
    Or all their sad significance—also
The latter hours of flowers and green grass.

What of the night? the night is sure to come;
    What of the day? we shall not see the day,
    We shall be very, very far away,
In a lone land, where there is little light—
—Let us await the advent of the night
    Here, hand-in-hand, and by ourselves at home.

Sonnet X.

AFTER the tireless night's monotony
    No choristers salute the rising sun,
  One would not think the day were yet begun,
Save that the dull dead-driven carts go by,
  And sad, ignoble shades of poverty
    Creep through the lessening darkness one by one,
Their weary daily race once more to re-run,
They do not *think*—so are not sad as I.

Thou dost best sleep—weak heart and weary eyes—
  This toil and turmoil have no part with thee,
For thou shalt be made glad by no sunrise;
  And these look forth to sunrise yet to be—
But through the drear dusk dawn of this chill day
A bell just rang—because some people pray.

Sonnet XI.
On "*Le Sept Princesses*," by M. Maeterlinck.

THERE is a shiver from the very first—
    Unto the cadence of the waves that weep
  Mystically clad in robes of white they sleep
And sleep, and when they wake, they are athirst.
Agony!—as tho' the heart would burst
    One may not reach them, for the stairs are steep,
    Yet one can see the sombre shadow creep—
A Thing one may not know—a thing accurst.

Alas O King! thine eyes are waxen dim,
    Alas O Queen! thy hearth is desolate,
    Alas Ursule I thy bridegroom comes too late,
And having waited such long hours for him,
    One hour yet more thou hadst not strength
        to wait—
The cup of sorrow overflows the brim.

Sonnet XII.

G OD grant thee sleep—child! if thou didst but know
   The weary agony of those who wake,
   Then on thy bended knees for their sad sake,
So many prayers from thy sweet lips would flow,
That God, who hears *thy* prayers, might ease their woe.
   Yea, God might even permit them to partake
   Of thy sweet innocent slumber without break—
Innocence lost, lost, long, long ago!

Sleep of the sleepless, this is worst of all,
   The swirling sand-wind driven by devilish drama,
     Hot eyelids only closed from weariness—

Oh! then, when sleep on thine eyes like dew
    doth fall,
  And angels lead thee to the flower-girt
      streams—
    Perhaps thou wilt think of them in their
      distress.

SONNET XIII.

> "*Diffusa est gratia in labiis tuis,*
> *propterea benedixit te Deus in aeternum.*"
> —Psalm 44.

EVEN as the apple tree among the trees,
    So among all God's sons my love is fair;
The shadow of sleep is shed upon his hair,
And his eyes listen to unseen melodies.
His face is like the morning light which sees
    The flowers that open and worship without
        care;
    All that the morning has of rich and rare
Is poured upon those gracious lips of his.

Ah love, thy lips I—but I can only pray
    That God may bless thee, seeing He made
        thee so,

    And let me bear the load of all thy woe.
So that thine eyes may kindle, and thou may'st
       say
    Unto the hill of spices I will go
Till daybreak and the shadows flee away.

Octave I.

ANY are dreams that one should tell thereof,
    But I have only one dream—I and he,
His arms wound all around me tenderly.
Treading on air, and flower-lit fields we rove.

Sucked down into the abyss of my great love;
    I think, beloved! thou mightest cease to be,
    And we, being made as one eternally,
Walk a twin star along the light above.

Octave II.

*"Ne m'eveille pas
de grace parle bas."*

LOVE! lest I wake, oh let thy voice be low,
    And very sweet and tender, lest I wake,
  Who fain would still be sleeping for thy sake.
O my beloved—I, who love thee so.

What worlds of weariness and worlds of woe
    Have fallen on my head—oh! let me make
      One moment of all moments—lest my heart
        break,
Say that thou will not wake me, darling, no.

Sonnet XIV.
St. Stanislaus Kastka.

OH! there are chosen lilies in God's house;
    Floods cleave before them, when with shining feet
    They walk upon their way serene and sweet.
The light of Godhead bound about their brows,
    They have not seen or known things riotous;
Nor could their ears bear aught that was not sweet,
It was the same, the cloister or the street;
    To them the serpent was not dangerous.

Oh Saint! my Saint! oh most divinely fair!
    How shall I dare to look on thy pure face?
    'Tis said thy countenance had once such grace,
That men who saw were moved unto deep prayer.
    Oh let us feel, who are faint, and filled with fears,
    The glory and the beauty of thy tears.

TRANSLATIONS.

Paraphrase from Sappho.

Φαίνεται μοϊ κήνος σόίς θεοϊσιν.

LIKE to the gods is that one who, my darling,
Sits beside thee hearing thy lovely laughter,
Sits and hears thy whole voice's chiming cadence.
          Oh but to hear it!

Love! thy laugh hath ever a silver cadence,
Oh my love! my heart turneth faint within me,
Oh my love! when I see thee but so little
          Love, how I love thee!

O and my tongue will well nigh refrain from
    speaking,
Love! fierce fire courses down my body;
Mine eyes are sightless, sightless my love, mine
    ears too
          Have lost all hearing.

O I am pale, paler than grass grown grey, love;
Let my madness seem bitter indeed before thee,
Since if thou leave me I were more sad than the
    dead be
                    Alas! oh! but what? love!

From Meleager.

Σιδωλον μορφής μάλλον ἐφλόγισεν.

I SAW Alexis wandering by the way
When summer cut the cornfields on that day—
Oh! from his eyes, there shot a sudden ray,
His own love and the sunlight; his array.

Torture of dreams, that night can not allay!—
Soul of a shadow, let me only pray,
That Sleep, sweet Sleep, who takes all cares away,
Will let awhile thy sweetness with me stay.

Mignon.
(From Goethe.)

Dost thou know the land where the orange
      blossoms bloom,
Whose fruit glows golden through the green
      leaves' gloom,
Where the winds are tempered through the
      softer air
To lovelier laurels and myrtles, flowers more fair;
            Nay, say dost thou know?
For there, even there,
With thee, oh my beloved, I were so fain to go.

Dost thou know the house, how stately are its
      halls,
With marvellous marble wrought upon the walls,
Where statues, strange and still, smile silently;
Alas, poor child, what have they done to thee?
            Nay, say dost thou know?

For there, even there,
With thee, oh my saviour, I were fain to go.

Dost thou know the way, the cloud-girt
    mountain way,
Where shadowed through the mist the lost mules
    stray,
Where dwells the dragoness and her dark brood,
And the rocks are rent with the everlasting flood,
              Nay, say dost thou know?
For there, even there,
With thee, oh my Father, let us arise and go.

The Erl-King.
(From Goethe.)

WHO rides so late through the wind so wild?
It is the father holding his child;
He holds the fair boy with sheltering arm,
He holds him closely, he holds him warm.

"My child, ah tell me what frighteth thee!"
"Alas, my father, and dost thou not see
The Erl-King crowned and clothed in white?"
"Nay child, 'tis the mist in the white moonlight."

"Sweet child, and wilt thou not come with me?
I have beautiful gifts I would give to thee;
Fair are the flowers that bloom on the wold
Where my mother weaves garments of woven gold."

"My father, my father, and did'st thou not hear
What the Erl-King softly said in mine ear?"

"Tremble not, be not afraid, my child,
Shall the willows not weep when the wind is so
    wild?"

"Sweet boy, and wilt thou not come with me?
My beautiful daughters shall play with thee;
They shall sing to thee songs, their voices are sweet,
They shall dance with thee dances, their feet are
    fleet."

"Nay, but my father, I saw the pale face
Of the Erl-King's daughter in a dark, strange place."
"Nay, fear not, my child, for I only see
The mute moon that shines through the
    willow-tree."

"I love thee, I long for thy lithe, living form,
Thy flower-like face, thy blood that is warm."
"Alas, my father, for verily
The Erl-King has done some strange thing to me."

The father shuddered, and yet more fast
He spurred on his steed through the wavering
    blast;
Onward and onward, nor turned his head,
For he feared, nay, he knew, that the child was
    dead.

The Fisher.
(From Goethe.)

THE waters welled, the waters swelled,
    A fisher sat by the shore,
His angling rod in his hand he held,
    Saw this, and saw no more.
And as he was fain to cast again
    With wet hair and wondrous eyes,
He saw from the waters cleft in twain
    A Water-witch arise.

She sang to him, she spake to him,
    "How can'st thou thus cruelly,
With tireful foils and fearful foils,
    Lure my children forth to die?
Did'st thou know how sweet it were to swim
    In the full floods far and fair,
Thou could'st dive in the deep sea, clear and dim,
And surely be happy there.

Oh I the sweet sun his shining morning face
    In my waters loves to lave,
And the mystic moon tireth not to trace
    Her path on the wandering wave.
Thou shalt see in the waters wonderful
    Strange skies of softer blue,
And thine own fair face made more beautiful
    In the everlasting dew."

The waters welled, the waters swelled,
    And covered his fair white feet;
A new desire his soul compelled
    So sad, so strange, so sweet.
She spake to him, she sang to him,
    And his heart grew over-fain,
He is drawn through the waters deep and dim
    None shall see his face again.

From Heinrich Heine.

I.

"Du bist wie eine Blume."

THOU art like unto a flower,
    So fair, so pure, my dear,
I look on thee, and my spirit
    Is sad and oppressed with fear.

I think that in benediction
    Mine hands on thine head I would lay,
And pray that God might keep thee
    So fair, so pure, alway.

II.

"See liebteen sich beide doch keiner."

THEY loved one another, but neither
    Would their love to the other confess;
They looked on each other so coldly,
    And pined in their sore distress.

They were parted, yet saw one another
    Sometimes in the visions of night;
They died, and their life was wasted
    Away without delight.

III.

"Konnt ich meine Schmerzen ergiessen."

I WOULD I could pour my sorrow
    All into a single word,
And then that the word as I spake it
    Might by the winds be heard.

They would bear thee to it, belovèd.
    And by thee it would be heard;
I think it would haunt thee alway,
    That very bitter word.

E'en thro' the veil of slumber
    By thee it would still be heard,
In the depths of thy nightly visions
    That very bitter word.

IV.

"Am Kreuzweg wird begraben."

BY the side of the lonely crossway,
    Just where the roads divide,
There grows a dark blue flower
    On the grave of the suicide.

I stood alone by the crossway
    In the desolate midnight hour,
It slowly moved in the moonlight,
    'Tis called "the poor sinner's flower."

V.

"Ich habe in Traume geweinet."

I DREAMED of you, my love,
   I dreamed that you were dead,
A sad, but not bitter tear,
   As I waked from my dream I shed.

I dreamed of you, my love,
   That you had deserted me,
As I waked from my dream I wept
   Loud and very bitterly.

I dreamed of you, my love,
   That you were still good and true,
I hardly ceased to weep
   My love, as I thought of you.

From Theophile Gautier.

"Connaissez-vous la blanche tombe?"

Do you know the cold white tomb,
  Where the breezes wandering by
                So sadly sigh?
Where the sad white roses bloom,
And a dove with soft white wings
                Sits and sings?

Sings a deadly melody,
Yet so sad, so tender, sweet,
                That in hearing it
You think that you hear a sigh
From the heart of an angel in heaven
                Love riven.

On the wings of music borne,
Something floats faintly by,
                Some memory,

Some shadow-like angel form,
In the tremulous sunset ray,
                        In white array.

And the nightshade as it closes
Throws its sickly scent around,
                        And a sound
Comes forth from the heart of the roses,
Sighs softly, as if in pain,
                        "Come again."

Ah no! to that cold white tomb
I will go when the long shadows come
                        Never again.
Where the sad white roses bloom,
And the dove with the soft white wings
                        Sits and sings.

And the dead soul seems to waken
And weep with bitter tears
                        When it hears,
At being so soon forsaken,
And calls to you tenderly,
                        Plaintively.

A PARTIAL LIST OF SNUGGLY BOOKS

G. ALBERT AURIER *Elsewhere and Other Stories*
JULES BARBEY D'AUREVILLY *Hannibal's Ring*
S. HENRY BERTHOUD *Misanthropic Tales*
LÉON BLOY *The Tarantulas' Parlor and Other Unkind Tales*
ÉLÉMIR BOURGES *The Twilight of the Gods*
JAMES CHAMPAGNE *Harlem Smoke*
FÉLICIEN CHAMPSAUR *The Latin Orgy*
FÉLICIEN CHAMPSAUR
    The Emerald Princess and Other Decadent Fantasies
BRENDAN CONNELL *Clark*
BRENDAN CONNELL *Unofficial History of Pi Wei*
RAFAELA CONTRERAS *The Turquoise Ring and Other Stories*
ADOLFO COUVE *When I Think of My Missing Head*
QUENTIN S. CRISP *Aiaigasa*
QUENTIN S. CRISP *Graves*
LADY DILKE *The Outcast Spirit and Other Stories*
CATHERINE DOUSTEYSSIER-KHOZE *The Beauty of the Death Cap*
ÉDOUARD DUJARDIN *Hauntings*
BERIT ELLINGSEN *Now We Can See the Moon*
BERIT ELLINGSEN *Vessel and Solsvart*
ENRIQUE GÓMEZ CARRILLO *Sentimental Stories*
EDMOND AND JULES DE GONCOURT *Manette Salomon*
REMY DE GOURMONT *From a Faraway Land*
GUIDO GOZZANO *Alcina and Other Stories*
EDWARD HERON-ALLEN *The Complete Shorter Fiction*
RHYS HUGHES *Cloud Farming in Wales*
J.-K. HUYSMANS *Knapsacks*
COLIN INSOLE *Valerie and Other Stories*
JUSTIN ISIS *Pleasant Tales II*
JUSTIN ISIS (editor) *Marked to Die: A Tribute to Mark Samuels*
JUSTIN ISIS AND DANIEL CORRICK (editors)
    Drowning in Beauty: The Neo-Decadent Anthology

VICTOR JOLY
The Unknown Collaborator and Other Legendary Tales
MARIE KRYSINSKA *The Path of Amour*
BERNARD LAZARE *The Gate of Ivory*
BERNARD LAZARE *The Mirror of Legends*
BERNARD LAZARE *The Torch-Bearers*
MAURICE LEVEL *The Shadow*
JEAN LORRAIN *Errant Vice*
JEAN LORRAIN *Fards and Poisons*
JEAN LORRAIN *Masks in the Tapestry*
JEAN LORRAIN *Monsieur de Bougrelon and Other Stories*
JEAN LORRAIN *Nightmares of an Ether-Drinker*
JEAN LORRAIN
The Soul-Drinker and Other Decadent Fantasies
ARTHUR MACHEN *N*
ARTHUR MACHEN *Ornaments in Jade*
CAMILLE MAUCLAIR *The Frail Soul and Other Stories*
CATULLE MENDÈS *Bluebirds*
CATULLE MENDÈS *For Reading in the Bath*
CATULLE MENDÈS *Mephistophela*
ÉPHRAÏM MIKHAËL *Halyartes and Other Poems in Prose*
LUIS DE MIRANDA *Who Killed the Poet?*
OCTAVE MIRBEAU *The Death of Balzac*
TERESA WILMS MONTT *In the Stillness of Marble*
TERESA WILMS MONTT *Sentimental Doubts*
CHARLES MORICE *Babels, Balloons and Innocent Eyes*
DAMIAN MURPHY *Daughters of Apostasy*
DAMIAN MURPHY *The Star of Gnosia*
KRISTINE ONG MUSLIM *Butterfly Dream*
PHILOTHÉE O'NEDDY *The Enchanted Ring*
YARROW PAISLEY *Mendicant City*
URSULA PFLUG *Down From*
ADOLPHE RETTÉ *Misty Thule*
JEAN RICHEPIN *The Bull-Man and the Grasshopper*

DAVID RIX *A Blast of Hunters*
FREDERICK ROLFE (Baron Corvo) *Amico di Sandro*
FREDERICK ROLFE (Baron Corvo)
   An Ossuary of the North Lagoon and Other Stories
JASON ROLFE *An Archive of Human Nonsense*
ROBERT SCHEFFER *Prince Narcissus and Other Stories*
BRIAN STABLEFORD (editor)
   Decadence and Symbolism: A Showcase Anthology
BRIAN STABLEFORD (editor) *The Snuggly Satyricon*
BRIAN STABLEFORD *The Insubstantial Pageant*
BRIAN STABLEFORD *Spirits of the Vasty Deep*
BRIAN STABLEFORD *The Truths of Darkness*
COUNT ERIC STENBOCK *Love, Sleep & Dreams*
COUNT ERIC STENBOCK *Myrtle, Rue & Cypress*
COUNT ERIC STENBOCK *Studies of Death*
MONTAGUE SUMMERS *The Bride of Christ and Other Fictions*
GILBERT-AUGUSTIN THIERRY *Reincarnation and Redemption*
DOUGLAS THOMPSON *The Fallen West*
TOADHOUSE *Gone Fishing with Samy Rosenstock*
TOADHOUSE *Living and Dying in a Mind Field*
RUGGERO VASARI *Raun*
JANE DE LA VAUDÈRE *The Demi-Sexes and The Androgynes*
JANE DE LA VAUDÈRE *The Double Star and Other Occult Fantasies*
JANE DE LA VAUDÈRE *The Mystery of Kama and Brahma's Courtesans*
JANE DE LA VAUDÈRE *The Priestesses of Mylitta*
JANE DE LA VAUDÈRE *Syta's Harem and Pharaoh's Lover*
JANE DE LA VAUDÈRE *Three Flowers and The King of Siam's Amazon*
JANE DE LA VAUDÈRE *The Witch of Ecbatana and The Virgin of Israel*
AUGUSTE VILLIERS DE L'ISLE-ADAM *Isis*
RENÉE VIVIEN AND HÉLÈNE DE ZUYLEN DE NYEVELT
   Faustina and Other Stories
RENÉE VIVIEN *Lilith's Legacy*
RENÉE VIVIEN *A Woman Appeared to Me*
KAREL VAN DE WOESTIJNE *The Dying Peasant*

www.ingramcontent.com/pod-product-compliance
Lightning Source LLC
Chambersburg PA
CBHW060459080526
44584CB00015B/1486